The Story of
CHOCOLATE

THIS EDITION
Produced for DK by WonderLab Group LLC
Jennifer Emmett, Erica Green, Kate Hale, *Founders*

Editor Maya Myers; **Photography Editor** Kelley Miller; **Managing Editor** Rachel Houghton;
Designers Project Design Company; **Researcher** Michelle Harris; **Copy Editor** Lori Merritt;
Indexer Connie Binder; **Proofreader** Susan K. Hom; **Series Reading Specialist** Dr. Jennifer Albro;
Sensitivity Reader Ebonye Gussine Wilkins

First American Edition, 2025
Published in the United States by DK Publishing, a division of Penguin Random House LLC
1745 Broadway, 20th Floor, New York, NY 10019

Copyright © 2025 Dorling Kindersley Limited
24 25 26 27 10 9 8 7 6 5 4 3 2 1
001–345401–April/2025

All rights reserved.
Without limiting the rights under the copyright reserved above, no part of this publication may be reproduced, stored in or introduced into a retrieval system, or transmitted, in any form, or by any means (electronic, mechanical, photocopying, recording, or otherwise), without the prior written permission of the copyright owner.
Published in Great Britain by Dorling Kindersley Limited

A catalog record for this book is available from the Library of Congress.
HC ISBN: 978-0-5939-6250-3
PB ISBN: 978-0-5939-6249-7

DK books are available at special discounts when purchased in bulk for sales promotions, premiums, fund-raising, or educational use.
For details, contact:
DK Publishing Special Markets, 1745 Broadway, 20th Floor, New York, NY 10019
SpecialSales@dk.com

Printed and bound in China
Super Readers Lexile® levels 620L to 790L
Lexile® is the registered trademark of MetaMetrics, Inc. Copyright © 2024 MetaMetrics, Inc. All rights reserved.

The publisher would like to thank the following for their kind permission to reproduce their images:
a=above; c=center; b=below; l=left; r=right; t=top; b/g=background

The Advertising Archive: 32b1. akg-images: 22. **Alamy Stock Photo:** Archivist 19, Greg Balfour Evans/© Penguin Random House UK (book cover) 44br, Incamerastock / ICP 23t, Minden Pictures / Mark Moffett 7t. **The Art Archive:** Musee Bouilhet-Christofle Paris/ Dagli Orti 23b. **Bridgeman Images:** © Brooklyn Museum / Museum Collection Fund 14bl, © Look and Learn / English School (20th century) 15, © Look and Learn / Peter Jackson 16. **Corbis:** 27, 38b, Christine Osborne 26br. Joe McDonald 33b. **DK Images:** Copyright Judith Miller & Dorling Kindersley/T W Conroy, NY. 42br, Copyright Judith Miller & Dorling Kindersley/Noel Barrett Antique & Auctions House 26bl. **Dreamstime.com:** Carlos Aguirre 35, Artjazz 29t, Yaroslav Astakhov 25tr, Aurinko 18ccb, Serdar Basak 12cla, Manuel Cruz 24, Czuber 12b, Farnaces 45tr, Anton Ignatenco 11tr, Jlmcanally 38tl, Kaiskynet 7cr, 8tr, Miceking 6c (Germany), 6cb (Australia), 6cb (France), 6cb (Netherlands), Sergiy Pomogayev 6c, Prostockstudio 28bl, Aleksandr Rybalko 1c, Pamela Tekiel 17r, Daniela Simona Temneanu 39cr, Vladimir Velickovic 6c (Ireland). **Dolfin Chocolat:** 41b. **Eric Postpischil:** http://edp.org/Germany/ Koeln.html/ Imhoff-Stollwerck-Museum 31c. **Fairtrade Foundation:** 35br. **Getty Images:** Universal Images Group / Sepia Times 13tr, Juan Silva 43b. **Getty Images / iStock:** E+ / PamelaJoeMcFarlane 4-5, Everyday better to do everything you love 13b, 18crb, Media Lens King 36, Mrtekmekci 10, NNehring 20-21, Pannonia 28cr, Seastock 32-33. **Grenada Chocolate Company:** 39b.
Karen Robinson: 37b. **Kobal Collection:** Warner Bros 45b. **Lindt & Sprungli (International) AG:** 42t.
Lonely Planet Images: Greg Elms 44cl. **Plamil Foods Ltd:** 37tl. **Photolibrary.com:** Paul Poplis 40br. **Reuters:** 6b.
Shutterstock.com: DW art 9, Gianni Dagli Orti 11b. **Topfoto.co.uk:** 8b.

Cover images: *Front:* **Dreamstime.com:** Chernetskaya c, Narong Khueankaew b.
Back: **Dreamstime.com:** Microvone (tl), (cla), Vladimir Yudin cl

www.dk.com

This book was made with Forest Stewardship Council™ certified paper – one small step in DK's commitment to a sustainable future.
Learn more at www.dk.com/uk/ information/sustainability

Level 3

The Story of
CHOCOLATE

C. J. Polin and Rose Davidson

Contents

6 Chocolate Trees

10 An Ancient Treat

16 To Europe and Beyond

26 Chocolate Factories

34 Making Chocolate Today

44 All Kinds of Chocolate

46 Glossary

47 Index

48 Quiz

Chocolate Trees

Do you like chocolate? Many people do! Where does chocolate come from? And how is it made into the sweet, delicious treats we love to eat? The history behind these answers is not always as sweet as you might think.

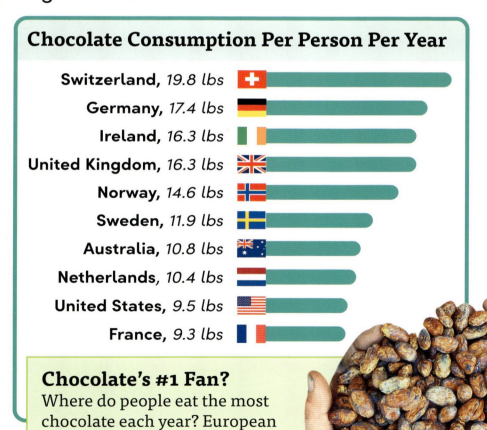

Chocolate Consumption Per Person Per Year

- Switzerland, *19.8 lbs*
- Germany, *17.4 lbs*
- Ireland, *16.3 lbs*
- United Kingdom, *16.3 lbs*
- Norway, *14.6 lbs*
- Sweden, *11.9 lbs*
- Australia, *10.8 lbs*
- Netherlands, *10.4 lbs*
- United States, *9.5 lbs*
- France, *9.3 lbs*

Chocolate's #1 Fan?
Where do people eat the most chocolate each year? European countries top the list.

gnat

The story of chocolate begins in the rainforest. Cacao trees grow in the hot, damp shade. They flourish beneath the leafy canopy of taller trees. Cacao trees blossom with pink and white flowers. The flowers grow directly from the trunk and main branches. Tiny insects called gnats carry pollen between the blossoms. Pollen from different flowers mixes together. This fertilizes the flowers.

Some of the fertilized flowers will grow into cacao pods. Inside the pods are seeds called cacao beans. These cacao beans are the most important ingredient in chocolate.

Cacao pods grow to the size of melons. This takes about four months. It takes another month for them to be fully ripe. Ripe pods range in color from yellow to dark red.

Cacao pods are hard. It takes a lot of force to break them open. Each pod contains about 40 cacao beans. They are surrounded by sticky white pulp. The pulp must be removed to get to the precious beans that make chocolate.

What's in a Name?
In 1753, Swedish scientist Carl Linnaeus gave the cacao tree its scientific name, *Theobroma cacao*. The name means "food of the gods." It was well known that Linnaeus liked chocolate!

An Ancient Treat

Who first discovered cacao? Who opened these giant pods to find beans? And who figured out the beans could be used to make such a delicious treat?

Cacao trees grow near the equator. The first people known to use cacao beans were the ancient Mayo-Chinchipe people. Traces of the plant have been found at archaeological sites in Ecuador. They date back to 3,300 BCE.

The ancient Olmec people used cacao beans around 1,500 to 1,800 BCE. The Olmec lived in the ancient area of Mesoamerica, was in parts of Mexico and Central America. The Olmec fermented the beans. Then, they roasted them and ground them up. They used the ground beans to make a beverage.

The ancient Maya also lived in Mesoamerica. The Maya were among the first people to plant cacao beans, around the eighth century. They used the beans as money.

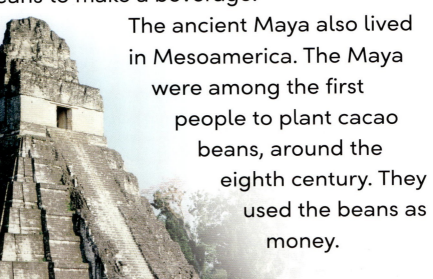

Ruins of the ancient Maya Temple of the Giant Jaguar, Tikal, Guatemala

11

Aztec lands were too dry to grow cacao trees. The Maya traded cacao beans to the Aztec people. By the 1500s, the Aztec were drinking cacao every day. Like the Maya, they made a spicy cacao drink. They mixed ground cacao beans with ground chilies. The mixture was poured back and forth between two jugs. Then, it could be poured from a height into a drinking vessel. This made a thick foam on top of the drink. The drink could be enjoyed hot or cold.

ground chilies

ground cacao beans

Cacao beans are not sweet. Without added sweetener, the taste is very bitter. In fact, some of the names used for the drink were chocolatl, xocolatl, and chocolhaa. These names are said to mean "bitter water." Sometimes, though, the Maya and the Aztec flavored their cacao drinks with honey.

A Maya drinking cup made in Guatemala around the 8th century CE

The Maya and Aztec believed cacao was a gift from the gods. It was served at many important events, including weddings and funerals. They also used cacao as medicine. It was used to treat ailments such as stomachaches and indigestion.

13

Army Food Supplies
Some of Moctezuma II's cacao beans were made into wafers for his army. This was an early type of instant cocoa mix.

In the 15th century, the Aztec expanded their territory. When they conquered a new region, they demanded taxes from the people there. The people paid the taxes in the form of cacao beans.

Aztec kings filled storehouses with the valuable beans. Aztec emperor Moctezuma II was believed to have more than 960 million beans in his storehouses. He reportedly drank some 50 goblets of cacao per day.

By the early 16th century, cacao farms were thriving along riverbanks in Mesoamerica. But soon, European invaders would arrive. They would want to claim the cacao farms for themselves.

Aztec figure holding cacao pod

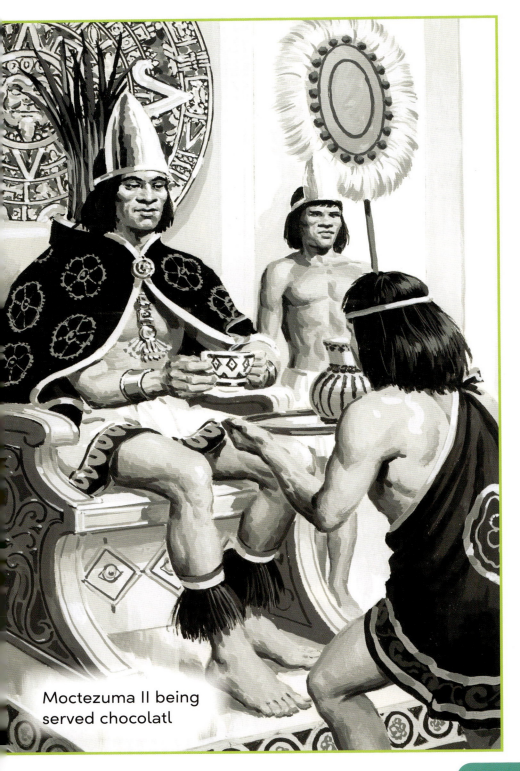
Moctezuma II being served chocolatl

To Europe and Beyond

In 1519, Spanish explorer Hernán Cortés arrived in what is now Mexico. The Aztec emperor Moctezuma II welcomed Cortés with a feast featuring chocolatl.
But Cortés had come to claim the land—and the cacao farms—for Spain.

Cortés imprisoned the Aztec emperor and attempted to rule the Aztec people. Soon, the Spanish and the Aztec were at war. By 1521, Cortés had conquered the Aztec. He took over their land. The Aztec were forced to give their cacao to the Spanish.

The Spanish took cacao to the islands now known as Trinidad and Tobago. These islands were part of the Spanish empire. They enslaved Indigenous people there to farm the cacao.

By the 1600s, many people from Africa were brought to the islands. They were enslaved there. They were forced to work hard for no pay. The Spanish created more cacao farms. The enslaved people had to tend the trees and harvest the crops.

Cacao beans were brought to Spain. There, people started adding sugar to create a sweeter taste. This new form of the drink became a favorite delicacy.

Chocolatl was popular among the noble classes. Both cacao beans and sugar had to be imported from the Americas. This made chocolate a luxury only the rich could afford. It was also said to be good for your health. This increased demand for the rare product.

16th-century Spanish nobles

In Mesoamerica, Spanish invaders continued to grow cacao trees. There was a lot of money to be made by growing cacao. The Spanish wanted to keep the money for themselves.

Here, too, the Spanish enslaved the Indigenous people of the area. These were the people whose land they had stolen. Indigenous people were forced to work on the farms for no pay.

Growing and harvesting cacao is very hard work. Many people died while doing it. In the 1600s, the Spanish also brought enslaved people from Africa to tend to the farms.

Cacao beans were in short supply in Europe. The Spanish kept chocolate to themselves. They loved the drink and didn't want others to use the beans. It took nearly 100 years for the secret to spread to other parts of Europe.

By the 1650s, people in London were drinking chocolate at fashionable cafés called chocolate houses.

Drinking chocolate in a café in Venice, Italy

In 1660, Princess Maria Theresa of Spain married King Louis XIV of France. This new queen liked chocolate very much. She had a servant whose only job was to make her chocolate. French nobles began copying their queen. They, too, developed a taste for the drink.

Soon, people across Europe were sipping chocolate.

Chocolate Pot
Imported tea and coffee were also popular in Europe at this time. Special pitchers were used to serve each drink.

In the 1600s, Europeans traveled to North America. They settled on the land. By the 1700s, Europeans had brought the chocolate drink to North America. It became a popular treat. The demand for chocolate was growing. European settlers wanted to grow even more cacao. They took cacao to parts of Southeast Asia. The tropical climate there was good for growing the trees.

Chocolate World

Today, more than 60 percent of cacao is grown in Africa. This is because of the climate and the history of colonization there. Côte d'Ivoire alone produces around 40 percent of the world's cacao. Other top-producing countries include Ghana, Indonesia, Nigeria, Brazil, Cameroon, and Ecuador.

Cacao was still growing in South America, too. Around 1822, Portuguese merchants loaded up cacao from Brazil. They sent it to Africa. This was another part of the world that was heavily colonized by Europeans. The parts of Africa near the equator would be well suited to growing cacao trees.

Cacao beans were being grown in more and more places. More and more people wanted chocolate. Chocolate was getting to be big business.

Chocolate Factories

In 1765, the first American chocolate factory opened in Massachusetts. Irish chocolate-maker John Hannon went into business with American James Baker. Their factory had a machine powered by a waterwheel. It ground cacao beans into a fine powder. This powder was called cocoa powder. Before then, most cocoa powder had been ground by hand.

waterwheel

Industrial Revolution
Watt's steam engine led to the development of new machines. This marked the beginning of the industrial revolution. Machines made it much faster and less expensive to produce all kinds of things.

toy steam engine

James Watt studying a steam engine

The same year, Scottish inventor James Watt built a steam engine. A steam-powered chocolate grinder made chocolate even cheaper to produce.

In 1828, Dutch chemist Coenraad Johannes van Houten invented a machine called a chocolate press. This made chocolate taste even better. The chocolate press separated the solid cocoa mass from the greasy cocoa butter. Chocolate made with the press had a purer flavor. It also mixed easily with water.

In the 1840s, J. S. Fry & Sons chocolate company in England mixed cocoa powder and sugar with melted cocoa butter. Before this, the cocoa had been mixed with water. The new mixture was poured into a mold. When it cooled, the chocolate hardened. This was the first solid chocolate for eating.

Cacao or Cocoa?

The trees and their raw beans are called cacao. Once the beans have been roasted and processed, they are called cocoa. There's cocoa mass, cocoa butter, and cocoa powder.

The chocolate business boomed. Many different kinds of chocolate were molded into bars and other shapes. Some were even filled with flavored centers.

As chocolate became cheaper to make, more people could afford to buy it. Cadbury, another English company, made chocolate boxes decorated with pictures. Children liked to collect these pictures. Chocolate was thought to be a healthy and delicious treat.

Until 1875, all chocolate had been what we now call plain or dark chocolate. It was also coarse and gritty. Then, two things happened in Switzerland.

Henri Nestlé was experimenting with condensed milk for breakfast cereals. His partner, Daniel Peter, suggested adding chocolate to condensed milk. They invented milk chocolate.

Four years later, Rodolphe Lindt invented the conche. This was a machine with rollers that moved back and forth over the chocolate. The friction and heat created by the movement broke down even the tiniest crumbs. The result was chocolate with a smooth, velvety texture.

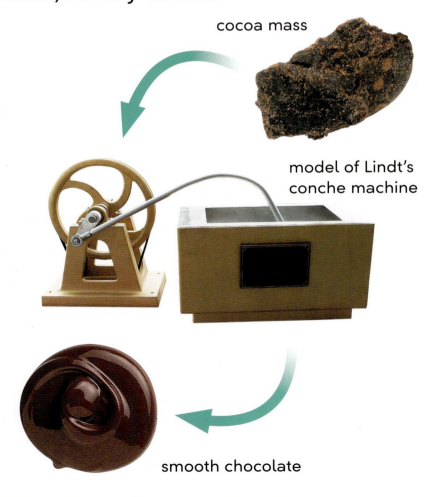

cocoa mass

model of Lindt's conche machine

smooth chocolate

In the United States, Milton Hershey opened a chocolate factory in 1905. Hershey built his factory in the dairy region of Pennsylvania. He could easily get a large supply of milk there. The Hershey factory mass-produced milk chocolate candies using the latest technologies. One of its early products was Hershey's Milk Chocolate with Almonds. This chocolate bar is still a bestseller today.

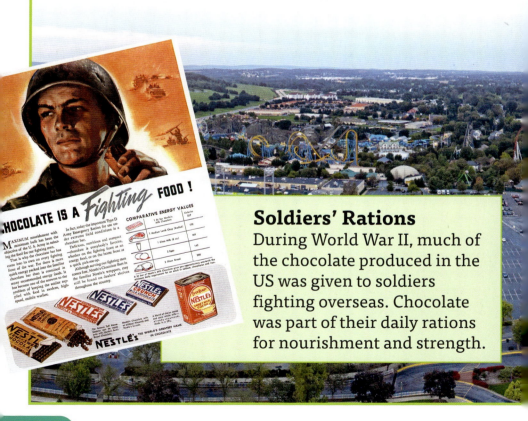

Soldiers' Rations
During World War II, much of the chocolate produced in the US was given to soldiers fighting overseas. Chocolate was part of their daily rations for nourishment and strength.

Hershey built a large, modern town for his workers. It had—and still has—a hotel for visitors, a golf course, and other recreational facilities. Over the years, tourism increased.

Now, the town includes an amusement park. Hershey has streets called Cocoa Avenue and Chocolate Avenue. The streetlamps are shaped like Hershey's Kisses, one of the company's most popular products.

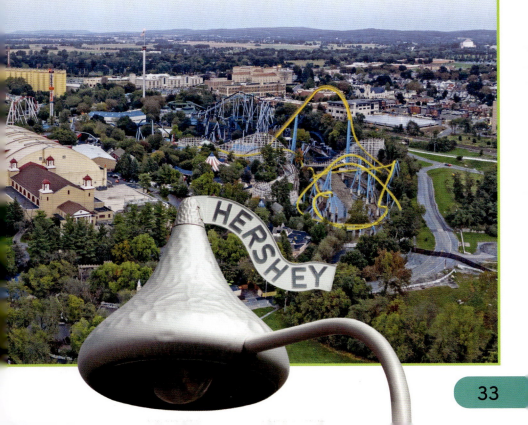

Making Chocolate Today

The demand for chocolate today is huge. To make more chocolate, people need to grow more cacao trees. Each tree has to grow for five or six years before it makes pods. More and more land is being taken over to meet the huge demand.

Near the equator, where cacao naturally grows, the days are very hot. Farmers often stop working at midday to wait until the air is cooler. Their daily tasks include harvesting and breaking pods, pruning trees, and keeping the soil healthy.

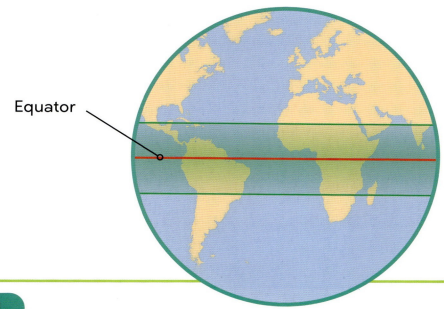
Equator

Fair Trade
Chocolate labeled "fair trade" guarantees that farmers are paid a fair price for their beans.

To avoid damaging the pods, cacao farming is still done by hand. Workers use knives to cut the ripe pods off the trees. They are careful not to damage the bark. Then, they split the pods open with wooden mallets. They remove the cacao beans and the sticky white pulp. These are the same methods the Maya and Aztec used long ago.

The beans and the pulp are heaped into big piles. The piles are covered with banana leaves. For about a week, the beans ferment. Insects bring microorganisms to the beans. This starts a natural process of chemical changes. This brings out the flavor of the beans.

Organic Chocolate
Some small farms do not use pesticides. Cacao trees are grown with native plants. This helps the environment. Chocolate from such farms can be labeled "organic."

Next, the beans are dried in the sun for a few days. Then, they are bagged up. The bags are shipped to chocolate factories around the world.

At a factory, the beans are cleaned. Then, they are roasted at a very high temperature. This makes their flavor more intense. A hulling machine separates the shell from the inside of the bean. The inside part is called the nib.

Cooking with Cocoa
Cocoa powder is often used as an ingredient in other foods, such as cookies, cake, and ice cream.

Only the nib is used to make chocolate. The nibs are ground in a machine. They turn into a thick paste. The paste is pressed to separate the fatty cocoa butter from the cocoa mass.

To make cocoa powder, the cocoa mass is ground into powder. To make hot cocoa and other chocolate drink mixes, sugar is added to the cocoa powder.

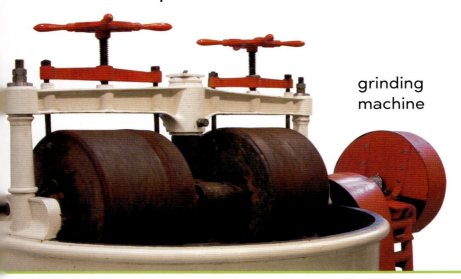

grinding machine

Dark chocolate is made of cocoa mass mixed with sugar and some melted cocoa butter. The mixture is ground up and then put into a conche machine. The rollers heat the mixture and make the chocolate smooth. Then, the chocolate is cooled in a process called tempering. This gives it a smooth texture.

White Chocolate
White chocolate contains sugar, milk, and cocoa butter. It does not contain cocoa mass. Some people disagree about whether it is real chocolate.

To make milk chocolate, milk and sugar are mixed and heated. A lot of the liquid in the milk evaporates. What is left is called condensed milk. This condensed milk is mixed with cocoa mass and dried into a crumbly mixture. The crumbs are ground up and mixed with cocoa butter. Sometimes, vegetable fat is added to change the texture and make it last longer. Flavors, like vanilla, can be added. Finally, the milk chocolate is conched and tempered.

Cocoa mass and cocoa butter are measured together. If you read a chocolate label, they are called cocoa solids. The percentage of cocoa solids in chocolate varies from about 15 to more than 75 percent. Dark chocolate usually contains more cocoa solids than milk chocolate.

Many chocolate bars are made in molds. These days, the molds are usually filled by machines. Some machines can fill more than 1,000 molds in a minute. That's 60,000 chocolate bars every hour! Nuts, caramel, and other ingredients can be added during the molding process. The bars go through a cooling tunnel so the chocolate can harden.

Shaped Chocolates
Chocolate shapes, such as eggs or rabbits, are also made using molds. For hollow shapes, chocolate is squirted into a mold. The mold is shaken to evenly coat the sides.

Chocolate is used as a covering for cookies, ice cream, and cake. The filling is dipped or squirted with chocolate until it is covered. This process is called enrobing.

All Kinds of Chocolate

Chocolate is a sweet treat, so it's not good to eat too much of it. However, experts agree that cocoa solids have health benefits. It is the sugar and other ingredients added to chocolate that are not so healthy.

There are many different kinds of chocolate treats—and they're not all sweet! In Mexico, a popular dish is a chocolate-chili sauce called molé poblano. It is made with unsweetened chocolate and spices.

A Sweet Read
Roald Dahl worked as a taste tester in a candy factory when he was young. This inspired his book *Charlie and the Chocolate Factory*.

Some chocolate creations are truly enormous! One record-breaking treat weighed 15,400 pounds (7,000 kg)—as much as 140,000 chocolate bars. But, like all chocolate, it began as some big pods full of beans.

Glossary

Cacao beans
The seeds inside cacao pods that are used to make chocolate

Cacao pods
The fruit of the cacao tree

Cacao tree
The tree on which cacao pods grow

Chocolate press
A machine that separates cocoa butter from cocoa mass

Chocolatl
A chocolate drink enjoyed in ancient Maya and Aztec cultures

Cocoa butter
The fatty substance found in cacao beans

Cocoa mass
The solid part of cacao nibs left after the cocoa butter has been separated out

Cocoa solids
Cocoa mass and cocoa butter measured together

Colonize
To take control of an area by claiming land that is already inhabited by people

Conche
A machine with rollers that heat and crush a crumbly chocolate mixture to make it smooth

Condensed milk
Milk that has been heated so that much of the liquid evaporates

Dark chocolate
Also known as plain chocolate, made of cocoa mass, cocoa butter, and sugar

Fermentation
A natural chemical process in which cacao beans break down, making their flavor stronger

Hull
To separate the cacao nib from the bean shell

Indigenous people
The earliest known inhabitants of a place, particularly a place later colonized by people from another place

Mesoamerica
Historic area of what is now part of Mexico and Central America, where the Olmec, Maya, and Aztec lived

Milk chocolate
Chocolate to which milk has been added during manufacturing

Nib
The part inside the shell of a cacao bean

Pesticides
Chemicals used to kill insects or keep insects off of crops

Pulp
The soft white substance that covers cacao beans in the pod

Tempering
Manufacturing process in which chocolate is carefully cooled to give it a smooth texture

Index

ancient time 10–11
Aztec 12–17, 36
Baker, James 26
cacao beans
  Africa 25
  America 26
  bitterness 13
  cacao or cocoa 29
  Europe 22
  fair trade 35
  harvesting and
    processing 8,
    36–38
  Mesoamerica 10–15
  as money 11, 14
cacao drinks 11–14, 18,
  22–24
cacao pods 8, 34, 36
cacao trees 7–8, 20,
  24–25, 29, 34, 36
Cadbury 29
*Charlie and the
Chocolate Factory*
(Dahl) 44
chocolate factories
  history 26–33
  today 37–42
chocolate press 27
chocolatl 13, 15, 16, 18
cocoa butter 27, 28, 29,
  39–41

cocoa mass 27, 29, 31,
  39–41
cocoa powder 26, 28,
  29, 39
cocoa solids 41, 44
conche machine 31, 40,
  41
condensed milk 30, 41
Cortés, Hernán 16–17
countries
  top cacao producers
    25
  top chocolate
    consumers 6
Dahl, Roald 44
dark chocolate 30, 40,
  41
enrobing 43
enslaved people 17,
  20–21
factories
  history 26–33
  today 37–42
fair trade 35
fermentation 11, 36
Hannon, John 26
Hershey, Milton 32–33
Indigenous people 17,
  20
industrial revolution 26
instant cocoa mix 14

J. S. Fry & Sons 28
Lindt, Rodolphe 31
Linnaeus, Carl 8
Louis XIV, King (France)
  23
Maria Theresa, Princess
  (Spain) 23
Maya 11–13, 36
Mayo-Chinchipe 10
milk chocolate 30, 32,
  41
Moctezuma II (Aztec
  emperor) 14–17
molds 42
molé poblano 44
Nestlé, Henri 30
nib 38–39
Olmec 11
organic chocolate 37
Peter, Daniel 30
pulp 8, 36
solid chocolate 28–29
tempering 40, 41
van Houten, Coenraad
  Johannes 27
Watt, James 26, 27
white chocolate 40
World War II 32

47

Quiz

Answer the questions to see what you have learned. Check your answers in the key below.

1. True or False: Cacao trees grow in bright sun.
2. About how many beans are in each cacao pod?
3. What are cocoa solids?
4. On what continent is most of the world's cacao grown today?
5. Which part of the cacao bean is used to make chocolate?

1. False 2. 40 3. Cocoa mass and cocoa butter measured together 4. Africa 5. The nib